Young
Rosa Parks

Civil Rights Heroine

A Troll First-Start® Biography

by Anne Benjamin
illustrated by Ellen Beier

Troll Associates

Library of Congress Cataloging-in-Publication Data

Benjamin, Anne.
    Young Rosa Parks: Civil Rights heroine / by Anne Benjamin;
illustrated by Ellen Beier.
        p.   cm.— (A Troll first-start biography)
     ISBN 0-8167-3774-6 (lib. bdg.)   ISBN 0-8167-3775-4 (pbk.)
     1. Parks, Rosa, 1913- —Juvenile literature.   2. Afro-Americans—
Alabama—Montgomery—Biography—Juvenile literature.   3. Civil
rights workers—Alabama—Montgomery—Biography—Juvenile literature.
4. Afro-Americans—Civil rights—Alabama—Montgomery—Juvenile
literature.   5. Segregation in transportation—Alabama—Montgomery—
History—20th century—Juvenile literature.   6. Montgomery (Ala.)—
Race relations—Juvenile literature.   7. Montgomery (Ala.)—
Biography—Juvenile literature.   I. Beier, Ellen, ill. II. Title.
III. Series.
F334.M753P3824 1996
323'.092—dc20
[B]   95-7599

Rosa was born on February 4, 1913.
No one knew then that she would
one day change the history of America.

Rosa lived with her mother, brother, and
grandparents in Alabama.

When Rosa was growing up, black people
did not have the same rights as white people.

In those days, schools were different for black children and white children. White children went to better schools. They had heated classrooms and new textbooks.

Black children went to school in run-down
buildings. They had no heat, no desks,
few books.

Black children went to school for part of
the year. During the rest of the year, they
worked in the fields to help their families.

Rosa's grandparents lived on a farm.
Rosa and her brother were lucky to
have enough food to eat. But sometimes
they were sad.

African-Americans were not always treated fairly or kindly. Sometimes they were afraid. Some white people, like members of the Ku Klux Klan, tried to hurt black people by burning down their houses and churches. Many innocent people were killed. Rosa's grandfather remembered these hard times.

When Rosa was growing up, she liked to listen to her grandfather's stories. Her grandfather taught her to respect all people, no matter what color they were.

Rosa learned a lot at the school she attended. But Rosa had to leave school to take care of her sickly grandmother.

In 1932, when Rosa was almost twenty years old, she married a man named Raymond Parks. He was a good man who helped Rosa finish high school.

They lived in Montgomery, Alabama. Both became members of the NAACP (National Association for the Advancement of Colored People). This group worked for civil rights. They wanted all people, no matter what color, to treat each other equally.

Rosa worked hard in the NAACP. She knew that black people were not treated fairly, and she wanted to do something about it.

On December 1, 1955, Rosa made a very important decision. She would take the first step to change things.

On that day, Rosa left work feeling tired.
She had worked many hours sewing at
her job in a department store.

Rosa got on a bus and took a seat. Black
people were not allowed to sit in the front
of the bus. They had to sit in the back. Only
white people could sit in the front. This was
segregation. It was the law in Montgomery
and many other parts of the South.

19

The bus began filling up. Soon there were no seats left. The bus driver told Rosa and some other black people to give up their seats for white people.

Rosa was the only one who did not follow the bus driver's orders. The driver told Rosa he would have her arrested if she did not get up. Still, Rosa would not move.

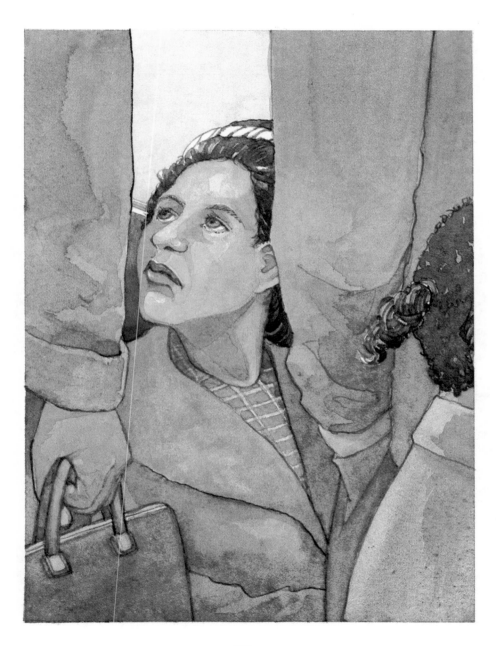

Rosa Parks was arrested and taken to jail. She was told to pay a fine. When Rosa was released from jail, she decided not to pay the fine. Instead she fought to change the unfair bus law.

Many people were ready to fight segregation. But Rosa took the first step.

Rosa and her friends organized a boycott. A
boycott is when many people come together
and refuse to buy or use something.

All the black people who usually rode the bus to work agreed to walk instead. This meant that the bus company would lose money.

An important minister helped tell people about the bus boycott. His name was Martin Luther King, Jr.

He told people to fight for what they believed in, but to do it peacefully.

While the boycott was going on, Rosa's lawyers took her case to the Supreme Court. That is the highest court in the United States.

Rosa's lawyers said that Rosa should not have been arrested. They said that segregation on buses should be against the law because it treats black people unfairly.

The bus boycott lasted for more than a year. Then, on December 20, 1956, the city of Montgomery got an order from the Supreme Court. Buses could no longer be segregated.

This was a great victory. But many restaurants, stores, and even hospitals were still not open to African-Americans. It took many years, and many battles, to end segregation.

Rosa Parks has worked hard for the civil rights movement. She has many honors and awards for all that she has done. But one right stands before them all—the right to be treated fairly and with respect.